The Chick
at the Back
of the Church

Some poems in *The Chick at the Back of the Church* have previously appeared or will appear in the following periodicals:

Canada: *The Alchemist; The Antigonish Review; Canadian Dimension; Canadian Forum; Contemporary Verse 2; Event; Fireweed; Geist; The New Quarterly; Prism International; Quarry; sub-Terrain; This; TickleAce; Transitions; Women's Education Des Femmes; The Windsor Review; Zygote*

USA: *Atom Mind; The Cathartic; The Cincinnati Poets Collective; Curriculum Vitae; The Home Planet News; Potpourri; Spoon River Poetry Review*

England: *The Frogmore Papers; Orbis; The Rialto*

Ireland: *Poetry Ireland Review*

Wales: *Planet, The Welsh Internationalist*

Australia: *Bystander; Going Down Swinging; Imago; Verandah*

Anthologies: *The Edges of Time* (Seraphim Editions); *Hammer and Tongs* (Smoking Lung Press); *Lady Driven* (Seven Sisters Publishing); *Love Poems for the Media Age* (Ripple Effect Press); *Meltwater* (The Banff Centre Press); *Northwest Edge: Deviant Fictions* (two girls press); *In Our Own Words 1* (MWE Enterprises); *In Our Own Words 2* (MWE Enterprises); *Netherworlds* (Ripple Effect Press); *Seven Sisters* (Permanent Press); *Vintage 95* (League of Canadian Poets)

The Chick
at the Back
of the Church

Billie Livingston

NIGHTWOOD EDITIONS

Nightwood Editions
R.R. #22, 3692 Beach Avenue
Roberts Creek, BC
Canada V0N 2W2

THE CANADA COUNCIL | LE CONSEIL DES ARTS
FOR THE ARTS | DU CANADA
SINCE 1957 | DEPUIS 1957

Printed and bound in Canada

Nightwood Editions acknowledges the financial support of the Government of Canada through the Book Publishing Industry Development Program (BPIDP) and the Canada Council for the Arts, and the Province of British Columbia through the British Columbia Arts Council, for its publishing activities.

Edited by Lorna Crozier
Cover image by Ana & Joaquin Pedrero/ Fotografica Studio.
Author photograph by Joaquin Pedrero.
Edited for the house by Silas White

National Library of Canada Cataloguing in Publication Data

Livingston, Billie, 1965–
   The chick at the back of the church

   Poems.
   ISBN 0-88971-177-1
   PS8573.I916C5 2001   C811'.54 C00-911590-0
   PR9199.3.L59C5 2001

Acknowledgements
For their timely generosity, I would like to thank the Banff Centre for the Arts and the Ontario Arts Council. I also wish to thank Nightwood Editions for having the love and the drive to seek out poets and for bringing my manuscript to the skilled hand of Lorna Crozier. My gratitude also goes to the editors who saw many of these poems early on: Deadeye Tregebov, Susan Musgrave and Don Coles. And of course, eternal thanks to my family, chosen and biological, who encourage and inspire me each day.
                                                                — Billie Livingston

Contents

The Chick at the Back of the Church

The Chick at the Back of the Church	9
There Are Things I'd Rather Do	10
My Version	11
Ms. Muffet	12
Black and White	13
The Night I Slept with Charles	14
Old Underwear with the Tags Still On	16

When She Chewed Gum

When She Chewed Gum	19
Thrills, chills, and aspirin pills	20
Children's Aid Is Coming	22
Confiscation	24
She Came Home for Awhile	25
Marilyn	26
At Work with Marilyn	28
Worrisome Shoes	30
Gin Wave	31

Crack in the Fishbowl

Crack in the Fishbowl	35
I Have This Thing	36
Auntie May	38
Letter from Lucy	40
She Has Eyes Like the Glass Ones in Momma's Old Dolls	42

Kitchen Talk

I/ Me/ My   45
Kitchen Talk   46
Boston YWCA   48
Positive   50
The Birds   52
Coat Hangers and the Ivory Snow Baby   54
The Conductor   56

What Looked Calm and Dark

Shedding   59
What Looked Calm and Dark   60
Paperweight   61
In Someone Else's Bed   62
Night Is Breathing Cool   64
Is Nothing Sacred?   65
Torch   66
You Are Married   67
The Three of Us Here Blinking   68

The Skeleton Closet

Glass Legs   73
His Third Wife   74
The Paternal Side   76
Fit to Be Tied   77
The Skeleton Closet   80

The Chick at the Back
of the Church

The Chick at the Back of the Church

Bet you could pick up anything cuz you got
seven fingers on your right hand and you don't waste
a single one. I read a wall said you rub
yourself to blisters back of here, soak
nipples in red wine and give communion. I like
you like that, Fearless Bitch, meet your maker
with your hands in your pants.

Can't help looking back through sermons
at those lips swollen like they've been slapped,
I think that's how you get them all
like how momma birds play wrecked for cats –
everyone loves a victim.

Bet you stuff smiles in their mouths, suck
voices from their groins,
lick wires through their eyes so they stay
closed. God help a piece that stares. I'm going
to light my jaws tonight so you'll see
me talking, click my knees like ruby shoes,
and find an empty pew. I'll lie back there
on varnished oak and quiet me counting beads.

There Are Things I'd Rather Do

Did you know at exactly 4:11 am, a train
passes through our yard or
maybe just its hoarse wail –
then again you wouldn't, you
weren't here to catch the 5:54 either.

At 6:01, I'd've slapped your sorry face –
6:17, I had plans to sit in your lap,
knock out your teeth with dirty words
but here it is, 7:27, and my silence
stuffed like a white rag in your mouth
has an ugly poetry all its own.

Don't think I enjoy this, watching
you tied to your chair by a single
nerve – there are things I'd rather
do than view an infidel.
And if you were smart enough
to lie a good lie I wouldn't have to;
I could peel off your guilt
and eat you like fruit.

My Version

First warm night that spring: college kids outside Future's Bakery, drinking coffee, wearing Gap sweaters; cars gridlocked down Bloor; you and me ambling behind, legs slack off bikes, till we heard them chasing through bumpers. Her with bleach-teased hair, denim mini-mini skirt, yelling *Lemme go!* to the guy stuck on her wrist, the guy in cement-battered oxfords, a man-size blazer on a skinny student body, voice hoarse – *Just gimme my money* – running right past our front wheels, and you beside me as she made it to the curb. A voice from the crowd screamed, *Let her go!*

She squeezed like greased cat through his grip, yowled *Leeme alone!* and turned on him. He showed his reasoning palms, *I just want my fifty bucks back.*

She shifted hip to hip. *No, I gave you your blow job.*

And every eyeball on the street jigged raw. *No, you didn't, you're a hooker* and *a thief*, he hollered as the cruiser pulled up. *This'll be a toughy*, I said to the cop striding past our wheels.

You slumped beside me, wringing the handlebars. *You don't wanna watch this do you?* and my rubber-necked guilt said, *No*, but I was dying to watch, dying to.

Laughing out loud when we met our friends for coffee, I asked them, *What do you think they did? Dust for sperm?* You shook your head, told me I was numb and wrong, it was sad and disgusting. For the last time, you told me that.

So you see, *that's* the night we broke up.

Ms. Muffet

Lying on my stomach, on thick blades
of Parks Board grass, I am reading
the same paragraph over
    same paragraph over
    same paragraph over.

The sun, swatting down on my head, ruins
my concentration – glares irritably off my page,
piercing, poking, spitting into my sun-weak blue eyes.

I am pushing myself up when I hear a *psst* –
low "s"ed *psst* – sound before a snakebite, and I turn,
see him there on the smallest swing,
jeans undone, smiling, jerking.

Blasphemy: masturbator on child's swing.
I can't leave – ushered out by that garter
snake. He *pssts* again.

I will not leave!
I refuse, sit up instead, giving
the view of my ass to the grass, I read
the same paragraph
    same paragraph. He *pssts*.
    Same paragraph. *Psst.* Silence. Silence.

Steel links jangle behind and I look back
once more to the kids' leather hammock swaying
empty on its chains, nervous bushes rustling behind.

In my book, an earwig wriggles
up the page, pincers tweezing the air for words.
I watch his soft self crawling and slipping, say *psst*
before I crack cover to cover, slapping
an echo across the baseball diamond.

Black and White

Seventeen and virgin, I sit on Cyril's lap, take up scissors, trim his moustache, lean in close. His breath held, I snip slowly, two hairs at a time, daring him to suffocate. His hands hover not quite near. At this distance, there is no talk.

Cyril is my forty-year-old guinea pig. Posing as an artist, he has photographed my face, breasts, ass, waist, clothed and not, black and white. Last week, he told me a dream he had: me, beach, mound of Venus smoothed by lycra; him, fingerbrushing over and over, nothing more.

He asks never to hear reality.
This is my job, to never say never.

From behind a camera, all can be viewed, but today's photograph has not happened yet. In preparation, Cyril irons starched white cotton smooth as envelopes. I will wear his shirt and nothing else. Averting his eyes, he leaves the room, "Don't button up."

Before I take off my underpants, he returns with a plan for the tails of this shirt. Like an intern giving his first Pap test, Cyril is careful not to touch what isn't necessary. He ties, unties, never grazing his fingertips or knuckles, careful not to open wide, never to look. I breathe his nerves. I am royalty, untouchable, perfect for the first and only second of my life, nipples smiling secretly like mouths of Muslim women.

The Night I Slept with Charles

Back when Bukowski claimed
to be alive, I read his work till I wanted
to vomit, the way he always woke up doing.
Sea-sick of him, I passed out, dreamed bearded ugly
smash-face dreams: Bukowski ambling into
my bedroom, me wondering, *Should I tell*
him how bad his stuff is? Dream-Charles had no
use for talk, climbed me like a beanstalk,
felled me and slipped inside. Him there on top
(which I wouldn't normally allow), my
eyes ran right to left, left to right,
too much, too close, like
the front row seat in a movie house. Lumberjack
chest, shoulders, gnarled old-man skin, he
covered me like the pea in a shell game.

He must be good at this, I thought, he
does it enough; I wrapped my
arms round his leather neck, watched
them change colour. Floating
under his barrel body, my arms dazzled
royal blue to Spanish red,
poster paper yellow. I'm a chameleon,
I dreamed, I'm a freak. He'll
write bad poetry about this. Maybe
that's how he gets laid so much, so
ugly: everyone he screws turns colour.

I wandered Queen Street all next day feeling
that grizzled man still inside me, minding
my arms until it was night and time
for work. Unable to stop my mouth, I told
the bartender, lender of Bukowski book, what I'd
lived through in sleep. He tossed bar scoop to ice.

"You did not!"
"I did so, it was sickening." He glared some.
"Bukowski died last night, died in his sleep," he said, *"You fucked him to death."*

I tied my apron strings, counted my float, then
smoothing his dog-eared cover, set
Bukowski on the bar.

Old Underwear With the Tags Still On

He asks me to remove
my top so I yank
its tight neck
over my head to reveal
my old bra (same colour
            as the dirty
            soles of my feet)
and my slip (same colour as
            raw chickens)
spitting up from under the drawstring
of my crepey old skirt

I've never been
to physiotherapy, he's not
supposed to be young, grinning,
floppy blonde-headed –
he's supposed to be middle-aged
he's supposed to be female

He assesses,
lays me down,
folds my arms,
leans across,
wraps me round
feeling my spine
before cracking,
his fresh young neck
near my teeth

Don't tease the celibate,
I think, feeling like
a dirty old man
in hippie's clothing
planning better underwear for next time.

When She Chewed Gum

When She Chewed Gum

Sometimes when I chew gum,
I remember my mother when
I was seven or eight;
      single, sexy, wearing
      hot pants
      deeply upsetting the neighbours.

She drank only beer or wine
in bars to be sure she got
her money's worth. Drank
from coffee mugs at home,
in case company
should arrive unexpectedly.

She chewed gum slowly, artfully,
      not like a camel like
      some women –
Even at eight I knew
when she chewed gum, it was
sex: raw, uncompromising.

And whoever dared near the lair
was made fully aware
I needed new runners and the fridge
could use some fattening.

Then weeks later when the phone
would ring I liked to chew gum
and smile at my mother as
I told them, *She's not home*
and I don't know when
she's coming back.

Thrills, chills and aspirin pills,

Mother declares – 'nother great getaway
　　'nother escape
　　　　from the landlord/ social worker/ phone company/
lover/
　　　Welfare/
　　　　　Children's Aid

Leeches, she mutters, take take take – they want my
money/ freedom/ body/ child and we run　　away

boyfriends/
　　sugar daddies/
　　　　stray men pay for
　　　　　planes/
　　　　　　　trains/
　　　　　　　　wine/ Librium/ wine/ wine

And we settle a few months
　　　– rest　rest

Welfare/ social workers/ Children's Aid comes
to　look　through closets/ cupboards/ drawers
for evidence; a man/ his shoes/ his shaving cream

Another new school/ friend/ fight
　　　– No riff-raff, she says
　　　I saw not I seen – It isn't not it ain't – Just because
　　　we're stuck in a sewer
　　　doesn't mean we're rats

Men and wine don't mix with neighbours
          – a social worker announces her visit;
          evaluation of my situation/ custody
          Rabbit from a hat! Mother has money for
          a plane – magic – last week we scrounged
          in her crumb-bottom purse

'Nother great escape
  – pack/
    grab/
      hurried/ harried/ we scramble into another checker taxicab
                              thrills, chills and aspirin pills

Children's Aid Is Coming

You try to prepare:
pick up clutter, wash dishes,
dunk your hangover in a mug of wine
until the doorbell rings.
The kitchen floor's still sticky,
your four-year-old is reciting
dirty songs her sisters taught her
before they fucked off and
left you in this mess.

In they come,
all smiles as they look
in your cupboards and drawers.
Dirt – it wasn't this dirty before
they showed up:
Kraft dinner toppled and
spilled on the shelf,
peanut butter and honey oozed
under their lids,
smearing their labels,
wiping themselves
on nearby containers –
behind them, the cracks and corners
have regurgitated every crumb
they ever swallowed,
spat them in the silverware drawer.
A ketchup smear grimaces
from the last cupboard as you laugh
nervously, mention again
that you haven't been well.
They move on to your bedroom.

You feel as if you are about
to be hosed down and led to a cell.

Until finally they leave –
and you lock the door, your door,
My house, my door, you whisper.
Your chest shuffles and thumps
as you rush to check the curtain;
make sure they're really gone
before you go back to the kitchen.
Your little girl pokes her head
around the kitchen doorway and yells,
Hi there, hi there, how's your pie there?
She gives a raucous giggle
and you gulp at your wine.

Confiscation

We were surrounded
by stocky brown bottles in cases,
empties piled everywhere. Some
who'd been sprung
sat loose outside
their cardboard cells,
waiting to be kicked to freedom,
to yodel down hardwood halls.

A chocolate cake sat
decaying on the counter
because I didn't know *tsp*
meant teaspoon,
day after day, on a chipped pink plate,
as disinterested drunks passed by
on their way to the fridge.

And all the while she lay
in the back room,
bubbling like old orange juice,
wading through DTs, wishing
them off the edge of her bed
those cops there looking for what
they can confiscate
like us kids and cats and we
just sat and rolled
beer bottles and our eyes
and wondered how
we'd get her outa this one.

She Came Home for Awhile

For two months I slept with
my sister – a refugee
from the foot of the stairs
her lover'd thrown her down,
baby intact/ face not

Half her size, half
her age, I patted her belly
like a circus balloon

Each night I sat
cross-legged and jealous,
on the bed, dumbstruck
as I ran my hands
over and over the immovable
ball rising like a sun from her body

wanting to bite it,
pop it,
scheming schemes
until she would reach
for my cowlick, pin it down
then swat it aside and swear,
soft and resolute,
I promise
not to love it
like you.

Marilyn

When I was four on Fourth,
my favourite person anywhere,
everywhere was Marilyn Careflower,
hippie girl next door. Long hair,
long as two Freezies, Marilyn, beautiful
Marilyn, who I would be or marry when I grew up,
sat on her couch with tiny pills, book, glass of water.
Dreamy-eyed job she had that day, crushing
yellow hard dots with water in her palm. She
opened a paperback's pages and smeared
the paste on words, line after line, page after page, giving
me poppy-field smiles on her dog-smelly couch; me
sitting knees under chin in one of her ponchos.
My mouth hung open. *Whatcha doin'?*

Marilyn – the only open-wide-and-tell-it-all
grown-up in the whole world – said,
It's for Jeremy, Jeremy in jail.
Hairy, bearded loverman of Marilyn Careflower,
in the bucket for god knows what, my mother said so.

See, I smear pills on the paper, take
the book to jail and he eats a page
whenever he wants to feel beautiful.
Could she possibly be smarter?
prettier? nicer? honester?
She offered me a pill, uncrushed.
Girl with kaleidoscope eyes was Marilyn.
I watched those flecks of green-blue-brown.

You'll see colours and love and beautiful
beautiful. Everything beautiful. I shook
my head no. My constant refrain at home,
No: No to beans, baths, brushing my teeth.
Now this, *No* to Marilyn. I fiddled
with poncho beads. She nodded, lips
upturned in her hippie-girl Careflower way
so I lay down, head in her lap, sniffing
the thin musky cotton of her Indian skirt.

At Work with Marilyn

Marilyn Careflower sold groovy clothes
in Gastown Boutique that year,
when she wasn't protesting Vietnam
from her living room. Marilyn
was a witch; all I wanted was to touch
her magic hair (ends past her bum),
learn to talk less, keep off her nerves
with my grade-one gossip.

Blue-beaded flat chandeliers rocking
from her ears, she made coins
and candies disappear with a crazy cool
flash of long fingers. If I'd known
the word, I'd've called her
heretic, hair-etic. Perfect.

Marilyn let me wear the cheek-pink poncho
from the sale rack one day, so long it dragged
off my bare heels and that hat, that one
off the window mannequin, wider
than my shoulders, brown as kid legs. *Go
next door and show Blue,* she laughed,
her giggles rushing down over
my face like water in Mountain Dew ads.

Next door was down the hall and I tiptoed
high as pie trying to watch poncho tassels
off the tile floor, walked smack
into two painted-nail, bags-on-wrist,
patent-leather-shoe fancy-ladies.
My hat knocked low down my face,
I backed, looked under, up.

Yellow Dress with Lotsa-money-voice said,
Huh, she looks like that little it *we saw*
down at Main and Hastings.
Blue Jumpsuit laughed downtown-luncheon chuckles
then on they carried. I watched after them,
came down off my toes, swore I would never be fancy
and never come with Marilyn to work again.

Worrisome Shoes

Her shoes were red,
red like impatience,
and they waited moodily
as she wrestled with her garters,
pushing pennies through
flapping faulty suspenders

she'd cuss and
eyeball her stroppy shoes,
push down the tight weave
of her skirt and reach a toe
toward the two sloping mouths
just out of reach, her feet
begged to be swallowed,
her ankles spat high, so high
her rear end couldn't help but
join in and jut out
like fleshy plumage

she'd slide 'em on
and slide 'em out
like dice across the floor.
nasty spindly heels –
not shackles but slick killers,
kicking her inhibitions to death
and doping her calves
into smooth smiles
as they sauntered
through bars prowling
for rent.

Gin Wave

after three nights like this
   spinning on jarvis street
      poor wet jarvis street trying to wash
   my head away   my head is way
is teetering
   shoulder-high is   head is
      dripping sky   drifting on my
         lemon wave lemon gin waving on valium
         waving for cars to slow   come in
      slow like the tide
can't quite make out
   their watery faces out
      through my seaweed lashes
         just little   just a little further
            just couple more pirates   irates
               sinking because
                  slinking below sea level
                     dragging hooks   opening my
                     dragging off my cold ocean flesh
               a little more   few more pearls
            and I can steal backmybaby backmy
               babies all the babies and swimandfly and fly
               to the warm brown sand

Crack in the Fishbowl

Crack in the Fishbowl

Riding a Hamburg city bus, I let my eyes glaze out the window:
people blurred on dogs on benches on shrubs; my ears catch
snatches of German. It's grey today, so much like Vancouver I
hunger for home, pang blue for rain hanging plump dollops from
fall-gangly trees.

We come to a stop, pick-up and let-off, and my eyes rest on an
old woman peddling her bicycle, full basket on her handlebars,
long grey curls flitting free of their pins down her nape. She is the
prettiest part of today. *Take me home to your ginger house and teach
me to knit in German.* I want to kiss her cheek.

Something rotten, a crack, a beetle, bites into her tire and rocks
her, slams her sideways into the pavement. My forehead, all my
fingers press the window. She crouches up from where she fell,
hand over nose, blood streaming through fingers like water from
a tipped vase, a crack in the fishbowl.

German-less, I am mute, gasping for air, for water. She kneels and
picks up groceries, cupping her nose.

Blood still draining from her small fine head, the accordion doors
close and the bus begins to inch ahead. Panic wells in me, leadens
me, just my mouth opening slow as flowers, closing, opening. A
young man stops on the other side of my glass, touches her
shoulder, helps her stand. We lurch forward; I work my jaws,
breathe through my shaking throat.

I Have This Thing

It's my mother. She says there's one other thing. And she pauses as if the Aunt-thing, the reason she called two and a half minutes ago was just a ruse, a lead-in for something she remained gutless to set free.

I've been thinking, she says. And I remember her old boyfriend, the one who used to say, *Don't think – please don't think. I hate to leave you alone for fear you'll think.*

I've been thinking, she says, *if you should ever find me dead . . .*

Uck. Must you?

Grow up, it's going to happen sometime. Just listen – and she begins to giggle, *Oh shit why did I start this?*

She clears her throat, *OK, let's say you come over and find me dead in my bed.*

Sigh. *OK, you're dead.*

Well, first – you know I take out my partial plate at night and put it beside my bed. On the night table. Right? . . . Well to begin with, could you put my teeth back in my bloody head. I can't stand the idea of them finding me dead and toothless.

She has some kind of Marilyn Monroe Death-with-Beauty fantasy. She would never dream of taking the garbage out before sliding a Barbie-pink gloss across her lips, to say nothing of the eyebrows she pencils on every night before bed, with or without company. She wants the cops to hover over her corpse and say *Oh God, why her, how can the world go on without this lush radiance to light the dawn?* She's sixty-three now.

OK. Teeth in.

Wait. And also . . . I have this thing . . . well OK, it's a thing. It's, well when I was going with – OK it's a vibrator. I just don't want – If you could just make sure that –

Oh. Got it: Teeth in/ Vibrator out.

Ack! Yes. Just put it back in my drawer – No! What I mean is: get rid of it if it's out of my drawer – Or in my drawer. The second drawer from the top. If you could just get rid of it before anyone else comes . . . Oh Christ, I hope it's you that finds me.

Auntie May

May's got a sad-on. A pointy sad, not
the least bit general. I feel its prick
but still no weapon in sight. Tonight,
for Auntie May's sad spell, I bring: martini shaker,
Stoly's, vermouth and ice, all wrapped up
in my ex-cat's basket.

We drink slow and deep, wincing less
and less as May swings from giggles
to darkness. Minor bitching
here and there but not *it*,
she hasn't said *it*.

I'll never get her drunk enough, extract
the thorn from May's paw, then out
it slides like a magician's steel sheet, the kind
they use to cut a lady in half, separate head from
neck, torso from legs – *I had an affair*
with a married woman.

She was from out of town – the saddest love
letters, both of us crying out long sad letters,
and hating our husbands for not
being each other; we were going to run
away. We were.

I wonder if it's all an illusion, if her limbs
are even real. She wiggles her toes, bends,
drops tears on them, says how her lover disappeared,
the letters, the calls, the plans all vanished.

I guess she realized first: I can't
move to New York and what would she do here?
Hank knows. He hasn't left me.

Taking Auntie May's feet in my lap,
I rub thumbs into arches
and use the voice I used for my ex-cat,
the tone you use for death and say,
You're still in one piece.

Letter from Lucy

I'm riding in the back of some guy's car tonight
high, feeling Jamaican wind play my cheeks
with a million   separate   breaths
that sidle
        down, puff my shirt like a sail
and patter cotton lush against my breasts
knowing back home it's December for real.

I'm ready to swoon
when my mind starts
rummaging through pockets for guilt.
There's a letter there – Lucy's – my father's ex,
the one who fawned on me,
envied my mother's luck having a girl,
who told her off for saying I had the uglies at six.

I can see her like I saw her at seven,
making peanut butter sandwiches,
backhanding bleach-blonde from her eyes,
cussing in the heat, talking sex
with my mother like I'd never understand, flirting
with cops who'd come to complain about me.

I read her letter on the plane over here, then stuffed
it in a pocket where I wouldn't be reminded
on my vacation. My mind is just now cracking
the page like fresh newspaper, reading
snatches out like headlines:

ONE OF THOSE ANIMALS
WHO LIKES TO BE ALONE WHEN THEY'RE SICK

Wish this guy driving would pick up speed – punch
the wind a little harder, whip

the page out my ears through the open window
to the sugar cane fields we're passing.

WEEK OF RADIATION –

Step on the gas you bastard.

THEY SAY THEY WOULDN'T WASTE THE MONEY
IF IT DIDN'T HELP

He's stopping at a red light, leaning
out the window, shooting
the breeze with a pal.

CANCER ON LUNG, LIVER,
I FEEL LIKE SHIT.

I sit tight, try to breathe the fat, hanging air
but there's peanut butter in my throat
and they're about to arrest me for stealing candy.

She Has Eyes Like the Glass Ones
in Momma's Old Dolls

If you stare in them long enough you think they can talk
then you lean closer because it's still just a whisper
and you try so hard to hear but you can only listen.
Until you see she's not from where she's born
she's a walking anachronism, a small piece of folklore.

Sometimes she takes your hand and quietly holds it
till the breath leaves your chest and you know she has it
and she'll hold you tangling above the rocks below
drag you down a dirt path till you're scared to know
what's beyond the trees you can't see for her forest.

But you run with her still, till she sets your soul to rest
till you can pull your eyes away from those glass lakes
those eyes that exude hot sweaty nights without a breeze
and iced-over grey ponds laden with slow thick fog
calling children you can never reach over the dreamers' wall.

Then when you feel the strength at last to look back
she's already wandered halfway to the back door
leaving your hands cold, your tongue too swollen to speak.

Kitchen Talk

I/ Me/ My

Her mind is knotting words together
like *nice, pretty, good, wife.*
Other words begin to straddle them:
no, angry, why?
New words like
I, Me, My.

Forty-five and afraid to speak.
Numbness oozes through her body
like cake batter thickening in the heat.
Her hands lie palms up
in her lap, waiting.

Six hours till children, eight hours
to say *I, Me, My.*

Her silence waits to be pummelled
into sound; the secret film
begins to run in her brain,
and her hands come alive with his hair
gripped in her fingers.
She hears his head striking pavement,
feels the weight of his skull
as she waits in her yellow kitchen.

Kitchen Talk

Poking at hangover food
(salty eggs and Tater Tots)
you begin to list
qualities you believe I possess:
Honesty Intelligence Bravery.

Fidgeting, you look away.
There is an aside –
having seen/ heard
pictures of my dirty-child face, my
Eastend-Welfare-Booze-reared, Sally-Ann-
child face, you can't help
but see me and mine (only
on occasion, mind you)
as White Trash.

The teeth in the jaws
of my clean-woman face grit
and my eyes well.
All washing, sloughing,
articulation, matriculation
is jerked away in one swift yank.
I mumble.
Something about leaving.
Separating.

You interject with
the drama of your suffering
should I ever disappear:
my departure would
blow a hole in your heart.
And I imagine the click
as I pull the trigger behind me –

a clean hole shot
through your breast pocket,
a thin cartridge of sunlight
coming out your shoulder blade.

If I leave now,
I will see through
you forever.

Boston YWCA

It smells institutional in here
this asylum they've created
smells insane like nerves and fear
and poverty
like fat and acne and found-lumps
under skin that doesn't care anymore.
I leave room 227 and try not to
shuffle like the others
to the disinfected tiles
of the second-floor bathroom.

Washing in the very last sink
is a ghosty string-of-a-woman
her spidery hands are scratching
one another's wet back –
eyes dart up at my intrusion
and I am unnerved
by that part of her that reads
Permanent Resident.
I splash and brush furiously
in time to my mantra: *S'onlytemporary*
and patter back to 227
   Pick your feet up 'n
  don't shuffle
  and don't
breathe in the slumping don't
breathe second-hand memories don't breathe.

I wonder where the Young Christian Women are
Glad they're not here
Avert your eyes – shun the desk drawer
for fear of bibles
The door closes heavy behind me

and I am faced with my room.
Pushed against the only
electrical outlet is the stick-width bed
its single flat pillow flashing neon –
We're not getting any.
Stuffing myself between tight sheets
I cringe to feel my limp hands dangle
over either mattress edge
and listen:

The tiny rasp of TV has scraped
under someone's door and is scratching
its way down the hall.
Twitchy and hollow, I force myself still
and imagine her face
radiated by a black and white box
sitting on that white aluminum stand –
I bet she's got the same one and she's
shoved the plug between the bed and wall,
jammed its two sparking prongs
into the wall's two slits.
She must feel smug.
I would.

Positive

In the Women's Clinic,
filling out sheets of sexual
history, I want to wrap them
round my body and head; prevent
my eyes from seeking, being sought
as I check off Methods Used:
Withdrawal.
I check it along with *Condoms.*
Guilty, Irresponsible – those words
slapped on like bumperstickers.
I flick at my insolent stomach,
dreaming the usual cramps and gore.

Papers in order, I hand them
to a woman who hands me a cup
and points to the door
with the skirt-wearing stick figure
and I will my body to pee
the right hormones – implore it,
silently chanting, *Bleed, Bleed.*

In the tiny mint-coloured room,
eyes sticking on the silver
stirrups on a mint cushioned table.
My brain leaps into the green saddle,
spurs shining and gallops away,
leaving my eggs behind.
Until the return of the woman –
Pregnant slips through her lips.
Jangling onto my file, it ricochets
off the ceiling and down into
my defiant belly, rolling over and over
until I feel the nausea I'd checked no to.

And *Partner?* comes next.
Business Partner? Dance Partner?
Partner in crime?
Yes. I make one up.
Because.
Because if I don't I'll cry and I'll have to
confess, admit one lousy night
with a gardener from California.
Tree planter, sperm planter,
all the same now. And it's
too late – tears; spring rain
on fertile ground.

Oh dear, she says in her Irish lilt.
Her name tag says, *Gertrude.*
Only a Gertrude would say, *Oh dear,* now.
Abortion? follows.
Nod. Yes. Of course, I drizzle, grateful
she said the word first.
How will he feel? He?
If he were sick, would you ask how I felt?
I want to say this. To feel powerful,
to be angry. But I can't be angry
with Oh Dear Gertrude. I'm too lonely
and thankful and

besides, the rain is torrential now
down my cheeks my throat and I can't speak.
Don't worry, we'll look after you.
Gentle Irish Gertrude
looks suddenly militant,
Be grateful you live in Canada.

The Birds

A plane-size dragonfly hovers overhead.
She sways in a hammock while
the midwife explains, *You'll feel a little dizzy,*
you may want to keep your eyes closed.
She opens them instead;
the hammock flattens, solidifies,
her knees are up,
feet resting in something like oven mitts.
The sound of the ocean has thinned to
tap water rushing over a doctor's hands.
She looks at green swinging wings
of the paper bug overhead,

still hears the sound of seagulls.

The doctor smiles, gently drying
her hands with paper towels, large
broad hands and matching shoulders –
She's broad
where a broad
should be broad,
her mother would say. Her father would
look up from his paper, say
Dyke.

But the doctor is her spiky-haired saviour
and drugs have made her weepy with love
for the anaesthetist, for the strangeness
of a midwife sitting by her side
explaining each stage, each prick and dilation
and finally the whirring as they shed her womb.
She floats, drug-dizzy with gratitude,
closes her eyes, listening to gulls.

The midwife tells her they are done
and she looks up again as they encircle
with their arms, raise her up.
A bullhorn cuts through
the jabbering birds: *Please disperse.*
Disperse immediately or you will be arrested.
Glass breaks. She hears toothy shrieks;
gulls are screaming bloody murder.
Sirens are calling them back to the ocean
as the midwife walks her down the hall.

Coat Hangers and the Ivory Snow Baby

Sister Mary Michael has us
marching our tartaned butts
up and down the pavement
outside Parliament.
She had time today
to make signs – mine says,
Stop The Killing
across a cut-out
of the Ivory Snow Baby.
I watch the building –
they're in there now,
gunning down babies;
blowing their little heads off
before lunch.

Sister Mary straightens
my collar, reminds me once again,
You were adopted.
Imagine if your mother'd murdered you –
cut you up and vacuumed you out . . .

I choke back
what I want to throw up
and say nothing.
She shrugs and heads
for the front of the line
just as a man steps out
from a stew of *Choose Choice* signs.
  Praise the Pope and
  pass the coat hanger!
he screams,
wagging a broken wire in my eyes.
The grade six class shrieks,
afraid for our faces.

He steps back into the other crowd,
leaving us to pull and chew
on those last words like toffee.

The Conductor

I've gone and played it again, Sam – said the wrong thing, said it
too flat, too sharp, said the thing that made your arms fly, made
fingers kick out from your hands like legs from a Russian dancer.
They pause near my face and I expect each joint to snap and
release – all five boots greeting the bone of my foreskull.

But your thin limbs confine their discord. I am safe with the
possible exception of the keys you rake over the soft pink of my
underbelly. Each word haphazardly falls and I am transformed to
a tearful roach, scurrying for cover, for fear one more might
punch through my paper shell.

Watching from a tiny hole where the rug meets the baseboards,
waiting, choking on dust from our unswept floor, I turn and
creep up the wall. You spin in disgust, throw open the window,
and rant at our weedy greedy garden instead. Rolling flailing
symphonies dance from your face as mad hands inexplicably
explain the sea to the trees.

What Looked Calm and Dark

Shedding

My friend's lover has just walked out on her and she has gravitated here to my broken grey balcony. I sit staring at the crippled limbs of my railing and push my big toe under chipping paint, browned, over the years, by the spit of tobacco-chewing clouds. I listen to her talk about him, descriptions of his mother's stiff blonde head, his bone spurs, his snake-like hairless body, his bad poetry and sallow, thin-skinned political friends. She turns the volume up on the radio when a particularly morbid wailer comes on. I suppose she's upset because she didn't walk out first. She doesn't say that, she just keeps picking off old paint, like the long loose peels of skin that shed the week after a bad sunburn. The same clean relief comes with each pull. She asks me if I have one of those putty knives – she wants to do the whole balcony, to be the slougher not the sloughed. I bring her a butter knife. I also bring a paring knife and an orange.

What Looked Calm and Dark

Is there a medical term for blisters left
on the insides of elbows, souls of feet, nape
of neck each time I need to feel you/ feel
need for you? Is this love or electrocution?

Downed power wires in a storm; we've tripped
each other's nerves. What looked
calm and dark sent sharking blue
veins jolting up our necks,
out our mouths.

My mouth. Speak for myself.

See, I can't love you
anymore, Live Wire, too
scared of the shock – the
sudden shudders, inexplicable
cries in public, in private
just as sleep is coming.

But all the same, you there,
me here, I dream your name
in the dark, bolt upright in that made-
for-TV way and know it's you
who brought me back to life.

Paperweight

As I come loose, I realize
that you can't do the job I need done
These papery limbs –
these onion skins of mine
need pinning by someone weighty

Look how rattled I am,
afraid the thinnest cough
will prove tornado-strength,
pull space between the earth and me

Sucked into its twists with such force,
I wouldn't hear my own screeches

Nothing personal –
you're just too flimsy
to lie heavy down the length of me
keep the edges from curling
and hold my origami heart
under the fold

In Someone Else's Bed

I lie awake under a rumple
of cotton and feathers, feeling the weight
of his ankle crooked over mine
in an effort to touch, keep touching,
find me through the fog of his dreams.

Alone, and feeling her
in this room like an aspirin
slowly disintegrating in my throat.
It is still her bed, I know,
as the smell of her curls up inside
my nostrils, down my throat.
I gag. Quietly.
Don't want to wake him.

Her ghost sleeps coiled around a
picture frame that is coiled around
her, coiled around him.
In the dim light playing about the patches
of dark I almost believe I see
her underwear trailing, silken, sulking
across their vanity.

Until now, and still now, his tongue
has found me only in *my* bed, my
stark white room, vacant of all
scent but the musk he found in me,
void of all sound but the insistent clucks
of my white clock teasing
yanking away minutes we had left.

In this room, the clock is red and utters
a reserved hum so that time
hangs thickly still and I am locked

in the circumference of a second,
alone and shivering on a bed where
ardour drove their nights into mornings
and that crimson clock cried out
as if they needed to be woken.

Night Is Breathing Cool

He lies languid along her bed, satisfied,
he is on his stomach, face
eased into the pastel of sheets.

Shafts of light nose through
small curtain holes
dapple pale along his cool blue back,
shuffle over shoulders,
down delicate muscles placed there
by youth as she sits, knees up,
back against the wall.
Night is breathing cool
damp breaths against her throat
in time with those she's watching.

Her thighs ache as if from a distance, as if
she were only listening to someone's description
and she moves her knees at such an angle
her thighs begin to shake
until she lets them fall
back to numb.

His body spasms in its reluctance to fall
through sleep. He stares round to find her outline.

Reaching for her foot he pulls it to him,
pausing his lips against her toes,
resting his head on them, *You alright?*
Is anything wrong?

Just sitting in the quiet, she says,
slowly sliding sideways into the mattress
and crawling back under
the sheet beside him.

Is Nothing Sacred?

What if Disneyland blows –
where will we go?
Into what big ears will we
divulge our secrets – whose
cricket thighs will sing us to sleep?

And what about now? Who will
tickle the insides of my arms,
make faces, speak in tongues,
demand answers from lonesome
balding spiders who crawl beside my bed?
Who will call *Bullshit!* into the screened faces
of all the world leaders I hate most?

Now that you've left, or rather,
I've left you, *Over* tastes too cruel,
and so I whisper *Later*
to the panicked gremlins in my skull.
I make disclaimers, make like
old Bubbe Clara, *"What's so bad,
what did he know from love anyway?"*
and wave my mitten at your sad
gloved fingers making goodbyes.

Torch

It seems to me that she is
rarely content with a man,
not content unless within,
creeping the halls of his brain –
she'd rather do without if not within.
Unlike me, a firefly,
a spark that vaguely warms –
she's got to be a torch.

I watch her slide, slick with oil,
in through his naked ears,
she begins as a smiling arsonist,
soaking his thoughts in thinner,
in varnish. Slopping puddles
of gasoline over logic,
then imperceptibly a chord is struck –
a match-like excuse for her ignition.

Tears blister down her skin
as she watches flames, like glorious wings,
envelope need and craving
with orange-feathered beats.
She slips out through his breath,
his mouth, the only door left standing.

You Are Married

Your eyes move so calmly
over the room, it is obvious
they don't seek to penetrate,
to thrust into me or anyone else –
they bounce contentedly,
hesitate frankly,
because they can.
They aren't pinned by guilt,
bobbing and weaving to escape
a matrimonial chokehold.

You are married

and it is new and enveloping –
a perfect gum bubble
of protection; rubber-sugar satisfaction
wrapped around your body.
Blind like a caller at the end
of a phone line, all words tumble
comfortably from your brain. Safe.

You are married

and so horridly
comfortable to be with
with your unobtrusive hands.
So goddamn magnetic
with your love-drunk smile –
that I could be drawn so typically
enrages me
and I am looking for a pin.

The Three of Us Here Blinking

Not quite midnight and streetlights are gawking
tall in my window. Somewhere
another time zone has you
just getting to dessert but not before
your touch-tone fingers rake this tuneless
jangle down my spine: bet your fingers fussed
napkin over corners between courses,
wiped themselves before folding neat,
excusing to the nearest phone.

I know because I know your ring: three times
then a blink; unending sure blinks
on my machine.

Mostly I feel numb, can't even
get a good guilt-on, believing
that blink is yours, red
with grief at the sight of my bare
ass in another man's hands.
I imagine you'll say, when I tell, and I will,
that I was too busy being

the self-absorbed, self-indulgent, self-self bitch
that I am.
Or no.
You won't say that, not the B-word. You'll clear
your throat, tell me it's unfortunate I've rejected
love and security (
S.O.S. pads and babies) in favour
of fleeting and cheap (
A strange wet mouth that whispers diamond down
my hip).

Suppose I'll humble,
agree

because I won't want to say what really this is: Carnivorous –
With him I'm no Kewpie, he's not afraid
to slam me to the wall, smile
when he tells me I'm bad and, just for now, I
get to star in
every hurtin' song they ever wrote. "It's all so gauche," you'd
say, perhaps, "You picked a fine time to leave me." So I don't
bother with you now – Instead I pin
his wrists, still
him with my thighs, turn my head
from your red and change my name to Lucille.

The Skeleton Closet

Glass Legs

Crossing the room this morning
I look down to see my mother's glass
legs taking steps.
I damn them softly, afraid
they'll crack and scatter
across the floor;
crystallized flesh in shivers.

> Last night
> my father's steel stared back
> from the mirror – steel blue
> sockets with a backbone
> to match and I smiled
> as his cool blood sliced
> through my veins.

> Last night, I closed
> my eyes,
> could've nailed anything,
> my life a game
> I could beat hell out of.

This morning
her dejection is thick on my sides
like fingerprints on a goblet.
I hear the clink of knees –
fear cracks if I run or jump.

I wrap my clear legs in wool, will
my bones to steel.

His Third Wife

I have come to see my father, see
with my own eyes the eternal
internal story of who cheated
on whom, slept
with whom, left
whom and when
amongst which whoms
this bastard child was produced.

I am sleeping in the basement
under the same suburban roof
as he and his wife, who becomes
irate at the mere mention
of my mother (the whore
who broke her husband's heart).

I rummage through their fridge
as she peers over my shoulder,
*tsk*ing at what I choose, her irritation
scraping cold against my neck
now that the man
who sired me has left the house.

She doesn't like to say anything
but it's her health – makes it too difficult
to have me around.
She forbids me to repeat her words;
my father is a wife beater. Shows
me splinters in the door as proof.

She's been watching him thirty-five years,
she says, watched him with his first wife,
eight months pregnant, both rolling
on the floor, clobbering

each other, and swore
never her. Watched him
with my mother whom
he cracked and cuddled while
she looked on with contempt.

She stands listless now, fingering
splinters in the door, *I just thought
it'd be different with me,
I thought the others asked for it.*
And I start to tell her he never
hit my mother and I want to tell her
I was bribed to come – tell her
he threatened to die
but these are secrets or
we're his secrets or maybe I just can't
sift omissions from the lies.

And it doesn't matter
because there's no room to start.

So I pack my things.

My father follows me to my room,
whispers hoarsely for me to stay, *Try
to get along, it'll work out, you'll see, just
get along,* as if we're children
not yet used to sharing
and he touches my shoulder awkwardly,
as if trying to form a hug from memory.

The Paternal Side

What happens if you finally
meet your father's family and hate them?
– Go to another country
to find words in their mouths like,
nigger and *wetback* and your flesh
recedes into your bones to
keep from touching them?

And they hack and snort
in the mornings, at breakfast
and mention how
the Vietnamese breed like
cockroaches, like the black ones
crawling up their own drains.

And there you sit remembering how in love
you once were with a man whose eyes
and skin would have sent them
screaming for a butcher knife, you sit
in the back of their Mercedes,
wondering how they attracted
such nice things in their lives.

Belching and swallowing
your cousin stops at the
light while a cross-coloured couple
walks across your vision.
He spits out his window and winks
in the rearview mirror.
If you can't have respect
for yourself, he says, *have*
respect for your race.

Fit to Be Tied

I

Grandad is the jealous kind, thinks
Nanna is playing the field at the mall
each day. Hard to have a wife
ten years younger, ten
years fresher,
longer, limber. At eighty-six, she is a girl.

When the cops come and bandage her
boiled arm, pick the kettle's carcass
off the kitchen floor, they send
Grandad away for observation.

Served her right, even-steven, tit for tat.

He wakes in the hospital, a groggy
prisoner, and resumes the fight: barking,
spitting, punching what comes near
until they set him in a chair,
fasten him there to keep him
from himself or anyone else. In the room his
daughter, my aunt, calls home, frantic that he's frantic, says,
Bring a scarlet runner bean; it might calm him down,
remind him of home.

Grandad grew dahlias and vines of scarlet runners
before the cops took him away, before they walked him
down the garden path.

We rush to the hospital, burst
through front doors,
running toward man-screams. My aunt
hears our steps and rushes us, *Quick,*

gimme the bean! runs it back inside.
We wait outside his door. Silence: his and ours.
Then *snap;* two bean halves sail past our noses,
chased by an old man's roar.

II

His kids have found Grandad a home: round-
the-clock care, all the best drugs – enough to keep
drool in mouth and fists in lap. And he's
calm – no need for blood pressure pills
now. They keep him tied here too,
so he won't get up, fall down, kick interns.

He will not be bathed by men,
he will not.

When I see him next, he is shrunken
two sizes, I'm sure, imploded;
only his nails have grown.
I watch my mother's wound, her
brother's guarded pleasure: *Can't
hurt anyone now, can you, old man?*
Mom sits and lays a hand
on her father's, asks him questions, asks
if the nurses are pretty. He
smiles a cloudy smile,
lets his hand be held in both of hers.
I don't know where to look. Mom

tells him how she used to love it
when he'd recite "The Cremation of Sam McGee"
round the dinner table. *Can you remember it, Dad,
remember the words?* He looks pleased as a boy
and begins: *There are strange things done
in the midnight sun by the men who moil for gold . . .*

my mother nods to the beat, holds her breath,
willing each verse from his mouth.

Once McGee is cooked, Grandad
and Mom duet: *Yearning just for you, that's all I do.*
My mother's jaw shivers as she sings, *Days*
have turned to years, smiles have turned
to tears and the crack in her voice
scratches at my chest
like a wet dog at the door.

The Skeleton Closet

In my closet, the size of a dining room,
skeletons line the walls.
Piled on the floor, mismatched bones
clatter up to the ceiling,
brimming against the door with such force
the windows have been boarded.

Sometimes I peer through the keyhole
to see how they multiply,
how new ones appear
that weren't placed there by my hands,
to see the dance, the seduction
that could spawn this mass.
To see if desires of the flesh
have clothed their dismembered bones.